1

Introduction

I t is my pleasure to welcome you to my Paris Travel Guide, a resource for tourists from around the world who are planning to visit Paris. Nash here, and I'm extremely excited to be writing this book so that anyone with a desire to go to Paris can have their pocket-sized guide. For one, now I will have a convenient pocket-sized book to give to families and friends who are prepared to travel to the wonderful city of Paris. Paris is a city that happens to be on everyone's travel list. You cannot talk about traveling the world without at least thinking about the magical city of love!

Even though it is not a very large city, there is a lot that you can do around every corner. The other reason I am excited to write and propose a travel guide is that the city of Paris has given me so much joy and happiness. The city itself is filled with many memorable histories from the past. When I see other travelers planning their trips to Paris, I want them to enjoy their experience as much as I do!

This pocket-sized book will not give you every last detail there is to know about Paris. I am simply here to deliver the most condensed

PARIS FRANCE TRAVEL GUIDE 2023

travel guide that will help you maximize your time and experience in France. This will enable you to have an unforgettable vacation, without needing to flip through 100s of pages just to find what you are looking for.

This book is not necessarily a book you read cover to cover. Rather, it is something where you would pick up the guide in the morning thinking" what should we do for a day-long trip today?" Then you open the table of contents and jump to the "Day Trips" chapter. Or later during the day, it is 5 pm and your stomach starts growling and you are getting a bit hungry. So, you start thinking: Which restaurant has a gorgeous view and amazing food? Open the table of contents and navigate to the most popular restaurants listed below. That is how you would like a travel guide to appear anyway.

Now, if you are currently still at home, and want to plan a trip to the wonderful city of Paris but have not done so, do not worry! Start from the beginning where I will talk about how to thoughtfully plan your trip, how to save money while traveling to Paris, the top tourist attractions and places from my experiences to visit, the most affordable neighborhoods to stay in while on a budget, and what to expect.

With all those things said, let's jump right in!

2

Things You NEED and Prepare before traveling to Paris

P aris, the capital of France is considered one of the most romantic destinations in the world. Hence, it has the name and is considered "The City of Love." There is no better word to describe Paris than magical. Paris has always been one of the most fascinating cities to visit in the entire world. It may surprise you to learn that Paris has its Statue of Liberty. You might consider that New York City's Lady Liberty was a gift from the French. What you might have known is that there is a miniature version in Paris facing the larger counterpart.

As the city of love, romance, fashion, and even the capital of the world, Paris symbolizes the relationship between the United States and France. Many names have been given to Paris over the centuries, each contributing to its image. Victor Hugo and Dumas Zola are remembered along the Seine banks in Montmartre and the Latin quarter. The aura of the city was immortalized in literary works and paintings. Through French films, every street corner is familiar.

3

Weather and Best Time to visit Paris

I recommend visiting Paris in the Spring and early Summer, between April and June, because that is when it is the most beautiful. It is also possible to visit during the fall season between September and October. In the summer, the temperature can get very mild, and there are not a lot of tourists in the area. As a result of the numerous festivals that are held in the city, which contribute to the excitement of the place, the weather is often unpredictable throughout the city.

In the spring months, you can expect a temperature range between 7 °C and 20 °C. During the summer months, thunderstorms can occur throughout the summer months during the daytime. Paris can feel much hotter as a result of the high humidity, regardless of the temperature, as the heat can be felt between 14°C and 26°C. On certain days, it is possible for the temperature to rise to 32°C. Visiting Paris during the month of August may seem like an inconvenient option due to the amount of tourists that may be flooding the city.

This being the case, I recommend that you plan your day trip accordingly. This will maximize the opportunity to take advantage of outdoor activities as much as possible during the day. Make sure you wear comfortable shoes, as you will be walking quite a bit throughout the day. Since the weather can be unpredictable, it is a smart idea to have a raincoat and an umbrella with you at all times.

Due to the fact that Paris is in northern France, the days get shorter later in the year in October and November. In order to enjoy Paris in the most enjoyable way, it is recommended to travel during the warmer months of the year. Please make sure that you check the weather forecast before you travel to your destination since it is possible for the weather and temperatures to vary dramatically there. In case you happen to enjoy the cold weather and are interested in visiting Paris during the winter. This is because there is no better time of the year than winter since it is the cheapest season.

There is no doubt that one of the most picturesque cities in the world is Paris. This is true regardless of the season. Are there any ways to find out when it's most convenient to visit attractions and what time of day is most convenient? When you want to go to Paris at different times of the day, there are many places that you can either Google or find out about from friends and family. If you want to avoid crowds, I recommend arriving earlier in the week or early in the morning if you are planning on visiting.

4

Paris Visa

The Schengen Visa is needed for tourists seeking to visit Paris, France as a tourist, regardless of their country of origin, in order to enter the country. Whenever you are looking to apply for a visa, it is recommended that you do so at least 30 days before your trip. This is because the application process takes a lot of time. It is also possible to search on Google and type https://www.schengenvisainfo.com for more information about the Schengen visa.

5

Transportation in Paris

From all major cities around the world, the city of Paris is easily accessible from a wide range of destinations. The city is served by two international airports: Charles de Gaulle international airport, which is the largest, and Orly international airport, which is the second largest. International destinations are easily accessible from Charles de Gaulle. There are several options for transportation to and from Charles de Gaulle Airport, including metros, trains, buses, taxis, Uber, transfers, shuttles, and renting a car.

In addition to trains, buses, taxis, Uber, and shuttles, users can also rent a car at Orly airport. Furthermore, Paris is well connected by train if you are coming from another European country. In Paris, the euro is the main currency. There is no longer any acceptance of the French franc in the country. You should not have any problems using debit, credit, or foreign exchange cards. It is imperative to note, however, that Paris is a very expensive city, so be sure to plan your trip accordingly. Consider booking an apartment or hotel near a garage or parking space if you are arriving by car in Paris.

There are various parking options available in city car parks. These range in price from €2.5 to €4 per hour, and between €15 and €48 for a daily ticket. There are numerous public transportation options for getting around the city of Paris. Despite this, you will still have to walk a lot, so wear comfortable shoes! Throughout the city, public transportation includes the metro, a tram, an express train, a suburban railway, a bus, and a night bus.

The whole city is divided into separate zones. For the city center, a one-way ticket costs €1.90. Prince of Paris Visite ranges from €12 to €65.80 depending on the zones that are covered and the duration. It is still possible to use a taxi. The city offers many other options as well, including hopping off the bus, taking a boat, riding a bike, and using an electric scooter.

There is a whole new way of discovering Paris if you choose to join a walking tour with a professional guide who will share their knowledge of the city's history with you in an exciting and entertaining way. It is even possible to take a free walking tour from some providers.

In the end, we recommend that you donate. Additionally, Paris offers a "Paris pass" that allows you to save money when visiting several museums and other attractions as well as skip some lines. That's pretty impressive, isn't it?

In the center of the city, arrondissements 1 to 9 would be an ideal choice if you want to save money on transportation costs. If you don't care about public transportation, the suburbs are a reasonable option. Paris can be enjoyed for less than 100 euros a day with the right planning.

6

Where to Stay and Cost in Paris

Among all of Europe's cities, Paris is considered to be one of the most expensive. Traveling through the city can be done in a variety of ways that help you save money. Most travelers stay in Paris for about three days and try to see the highlights of the picturesque city of love. While you can visit most attractions in three days if you do not want to be in a hurry, we recommend staying at least one or two extra days.

It is ideal to visit Paris during these six months if you want to experience the city as a Parisian. For you to see everything Paris has to offer, five days should be enough. Traveling to Paris for 7 days costs an average of $1,350 USD(€1354.46) for a solo traveler and $1,900 USD(€1906.27) for a couple. A typical Paris hotel costs $120USD (€120.40) per night, ranging from $68 to $422USD (€68 - €423.39). Typically, the cost of a vacation for the entire family will range between $200 USD and $450 USD (€200.66 - €451.49) USD per night.

Generally, hotel categories have a wide range of prices; these are all averages. Nevertheless, if your dates are flexible and you don't travel during the high season, you may be able to get better deals with a little extra research.

To save money on your vacation, find the most cost-effective deals that are cost-effective. Taking smart steps to plan your visit to a tourist destination will even enable you to save money during the visit.

The Latin Quarter, Saint Germain, 7th Arrondissement, 1st Arrondissement, Montmartre, and Gare du Nord are some of the most desirable neighborhoods to stay in. It is recommended to stay near the Louver, Marais, Eiffel Tower, or Champs-Elysees if you are looking for an authentic experience and do not mind spending more on your accommodations.

No matter what, if you are traveling on a budget and worried about expenses, don't. Here are some tips that can help you save money while visiting Paris. These areas are a bit farther away from where you can stay. Be sure to check if there is a metro station nearby so you can get to the city center easily.

The first thing you should do is take advantage of all the free activities available. Secondly, you should always order tap water when you are at a restaurant. It is also recommended that you take public transportation. In addition, you should purchase a bundle of metro tickets. You might want to consider having a picnic (or two). If you are choosing to explore offbeat neighborhoods (as opposed to just staying in tourist areas), then you should explore offbeat districts.

Paris is known for its fashion, cuisine, architecture, and art, which are all part of France's culture. During the low season, the Louver Museum is free on the first Sunday of every month. Discounted rates are available 2 hours before closing at the Orsay museum. You can save money at the Eiffel Tower by taking the stairway rather than the elevator. There is, however, a completely different way of life outside of the city of lights that varies from one region to the next. It is not difficult to find a fascinating attraction in the city of Paris.

7

Best Apps To Use To Get Around in Paris

There is a Wi-Fi map or Wi-Fi finder available throughout Paris that can help you find Wi-Fi. To walk, drive, and use public transportation, use Google Maps or Apple Maps. Downloading maps from Google Maps is a convenient alternative if you don't want to rely on roaming. For rides in the city, use Uber or Heetech.

Tap to find the closest water fountain, real-time restaurant reservation service is available through The Fork. For restaurant reviews, hotel reviews, museum reviews, and tour reviews try TripAdvisor and Yelp. "Next Stop Paris" provides public transportation information, tourist attractions, and e-scooter rentals.

8

Food Prices and Tipping

There are many ways to make Paris inexpensive or expensive, according to your preferences. If you are looking for nearby dining options with complimentary reviews, I suggest using Yelp or TripAdvisor. If you plan to visit a major tourist site, I suggest avoiding restaurants near the site. There is a wide range of coffee prices, ranging from €3 to €6 on average.

The price of an inexpensive restaurant meal ranges from €10 to €20

for lunch and €15 to € 25 for dinner. You can generally get a croissant for 1 euro and a macaron for €1.40 at most bakeries in Paris.

9

General Information You Find Useful

There are a lot of people and a lot of traffic in Paris, which is one of the busiest cities in Europe. It's easy to notice this when you're riding the metro during rush hour or visiting a museum like the Louvre on weekends. However, Paris usually doesn't feel congested despite its massive crowds.

French is the language spoken in Paris. Here are some French expressions that come in handy just in case you need to use them: Bonjour means: "hello/good day", Au revoir means: "bye-bye", Merci means "thank you", Je ne comp rend pas means: "I don't understand", Quel age avez-Vous means "how old are you?", Quel est ton nom? means "whats your name?", "You look great" means Tu as l'air super and "You look beautiful today" means Tu es belle aujourd'hui.

In Paris, drinking tap water is safe. Here are a few other things to know. Throughout Paris, there are numerous public drinking water points. The number of automatic public toilets in Paris ranges from 350 to 450. In addition to being high-tech and self-cleaning, most of them are free of charge.

Wi-Fi is completely free to use. A high-speed wireless internet connection is available for no charge through Paris Wi-Fi. In addition, Paris is quite fashionable. Therefore, make sure to pack up a few more outfits if you plan to go out to any restaurants or clubs during your stay.

For international travelers, if you are coming from outside Europe or from the UK, you will need a special European travel adapter to charge your phone and other services. I recommend buying a travel adapter before traveling to Paris. It is worth buying a universal travel adapter so you can use it in other countries too.

It is imperative to avoid travel mistakes that I have made in the past that could potentially ruin your vacation. It was the first mistake that I made. I did not check my phone to see if it was possible to put a SIM card from another country in it. Recently, I bought myself a new phone. It was a brand new one. Unfortunately, I wasn't able to change the SIM card on the phone for a couple of days due to the fact that it had been locked. Unfortunately, this made me unable to use my phone for a couple of days in Paris, which was a bummer. I would suggest you pick up a Free Mobile if you're looking for an affordable phone plan. This can easily be accomplished by heading to the mall and purchasing it from a kiosk at the mall, if you need it. You will be able to use the SIM card for the entire month if you buy it now. Approximately €20 is required for the service, which is a very reasonable price.

10

The Attractions of Paris

There is no better symbol of Paris than the Eiffel Tower. If there wasn't the Eiffel Tower in the city of love, what would the city of love be like? As part of a commemoration of the centennial of the French Revolution, Gustave Eiffel built the Eiffel Tower in Paris in 1889.

Seven million visitors a year visit this monument, which is about 324 meters high. It stands as one of the most visited monuments in the world with a height of 324 meters.

Musée Louver. A former royal palace, this historical building has an exhibition area of 60,000 square meters and is located in the heart of Paris.

You can take a cruise on the Seine. Discover the finest way to visit the "City of Love" while cruising the Seine at night. A dim light begins to illuminate the monuments as the sun sets. The front gives you a panoramic view of Paris, which includes the Eiffel Tower, Notre Dame, Pont Alexander III, and many others. With so much to see and do in Paris, your itinerary will be filled to the brim. There are many options available for you to choose from.

The Musee d'Orsay is a great place to start your trip. Get a taste of the opulence at the Opéra Garnier. Versailles Palace & Gardens are a pleasant place to spend the day. Get a close look at the iconic Notre Dame Cathedral. Paris will amaze you with its quirky charm regardless of what you choose to do there. There is no doubt that the City of Love will leave an impression on you.

11

Safety/Scammers You NEED To Know in Paris

E very visitor to the city of Paris is looking forward to having a memorable experience, and you will as well. There is a lot to do in this city. It is imperative to note that there are a lot of tourists, and there is a lot of money in this area. Whenever there is a lot of money to be had, there will be thieves and pickpockets who will rob you.

In this chapter of the book, I will share with you a few scams that you need to be aware of when you're staying in Paris. To protect yourself from them, you need to be aware of them. As long as you keep your passport and money for yourself, you don't have to worry about them getting stolen. So, as a result, you will be able to enjoy your time without ever having to worry about any of those issues.

Paris is safe for the most part but be aware that there are some neighborhoods you might want to avoid especially at night. The most critical thing to remember in all major cities around the world is to keep an eye out for pickpockets, especially around top attractions.

Make sure you keep an eye on your valuables and be very smart about it. Use common sense.

A classic way in which people tend to get scammed or ripped off when they are in Paris is when they are in a bar or restaurant. It is quite common for someone to run in front of you, bump into you, grab your phone, then get on a scooter and go off. This is when you set your phone on the table. That is a very serious matter that needs to be taken care of. It's easier to do this when you're inside a restaurant because it's more convenient. On the other hand, if you are sitting outside on a terrace, especially on the edge of it, you should pay attention to your phone. You need to take special care of it. Likewise, this is also true when it comes to the purse you carry around with you.

People are also susceptible to getting scammed via the gold ring scam, which is another classic way that people get scammed in Paris. So, let's say you are walking along, minding your own business, when all of a sudden someone is about 3 meters away from you, picks up a gold ring from the ground, and says like, "Hey I found this gold ring, is it yours?" Then they give it to you, and you have the gold ring in your hand. In response, you say, "Well, I don't think so." Then they proceed to ask you for money. They will ask you to pay them 10 euros or 20 euros. In Paris, this is a very common scam that is very easy to fall victim to. If you want to avoid interaction with them, keep walking and tell them, "no mercy." This scam is aimed at trying to get money from you by trying to get your personal information.

It is common for Parisians to scam you with a fake ticket, whether it be a fake metro ticket or a fake museum ticket, and these guys will stand outside a metro station or a museum and tell you something like "I have not used this particular ticket, or I have just purchased it and never used it, so you can purchase it from me for half the price." Let me assure you that over 99% of the time, these tickets are expired. This is a scam, and if you come across somebody who offers tickets outside the attractions around Paris, do not trust them.

It is also common in Paris for restaurants to charge a different price if you select an English menu instead of the regular menu in French. This is one of the scams that you will encounter if you walk into a restaurant and order an English menu. Considering this, I recommend that you walk in with an idea of what you want to order. You can also take the French menu and then ask for the English menu when you are ready. To make sure you get the right price for the right meal, it is a wise idea to compare one to the other. This will ensure you are getting the correct price. Another way in which they accomplish this is by bringing you a double expresso instead of a single expresso whenever you ask for a cup of coffee. There will also be an assumption that you wish for a cup of coffee.

As a result, you end up paying €5 or €6 per cup of coffee when you should have been paying no more than €2. Do not ignore some of those seemingly insignificant things. You must pay attention to them. You should, of course, stay away from tourist restaurants in the first place if you want to avoid this type of problem. However, you should first take a look at their regular menu so that you know what you're getting.

Among the many scams that are very common in Paris, one of the most popular ones is the fake taxi scam. As soon as you walk out of the station, if you're at the airport, or if you've been to any major attractions in general, you're almost certain to get people approaching you saying, "Do you need a ride?" The vast majority of the time, they're planning to charge you approximately three to four times the price of a regular taxi service. I would like to point out a couple of things that should be noted. The first reason is that it is illegal and the second reason is that it is very dangerous since some of these guys are trying to rip you off.

At all the big attractions, you will find what's called a taxi line. This is surrounded by a big blue sign that says taxis and you'll find a taxi line at the entrance of every one of them. If you are looking for a taxi, that's where you should go. In addition, all taxis in France are required by law to display a taxi sign on top of the vehicle, and they are all regulated. The taxi light is visible on top of the vehicle with a bright green light indicating that the cab is available for pickup. In other words, that's a legal taxi and it's fine for you to take it.

12

Top 10 places you NEED to visit Paris, You Won't Be Disappointed!

The most spectacular views of Paris can be found in Montmartre, an elegant hillside neighborhood. Montmartre and its surroundings are home to world-renowned artists who live and work there. Inspiration for Picasso and Van Gogh was found in the picturesque streets and atmosphere of Montmartre by Picasso and Van Gogh.

The works of artists are still being painted and created today, and you will be able to see them working on their next creation. It is the most iconic cultural and political monument, as well as an architectural marvel, that you will discover at the top of the hill. A visit to the Montmartre Museum would not be complete without a visit to the nearby church of Saint-Pierre and the amazing vineyards nearby.

Located at the foot of the hill, there is a famous Moulin Rouge, the historical birthplace of French cancan dance. In addition to being a very prominent tourist attraction, the Moulin Rouge has also acquired a reputation for providing a variety of music and dance shows.

The Hidden Gems of Montmartre: 10 Things You Should Know

The majority of people who come here just walk straight up the staircase when they get here. The few hidden gems that most people fail to recognize will, however, be shared with you guys in this guide. If you've ever watched a French film, there is a place you might recognize even if you've never seen it before - it's the Cafe des Deux Moulins from the movie Amelie. Tourists are always flocking to this place, so it's always full of people.

There is also a grocery store in the film, with the supermarket located uphill on the Rue des Trois-Freres, where you can find real-life fruit and vegetables as well as cheesy souvenirs of course. Aside from Amelie, if you aren't feeling romantic after watching the movie, then just round the corner in the park is another romantic spot called Mur des je t'aime - meaning "The wall of love is yours".

The metro system and the bus system can be used to get to Montmartre easily. When you are able to travel again, it will be possible for you to visit Montmartre as often as you like, when you feel like doing so. In case you would not like to walk up the mountain or if you have any accessibility issues, the funicular will take you up the mountain. In addition to that, if you do not have any difficulty walking, you are also welcome to take it as well. There are also more quirky attractions in the vicinity that can be found in the former adolescent neighborhood. Some of the quirky things are the vintage photo booth, the sinking building on rue Lamaeck that is a famous monument to the sinking of buildings, and this statue that, on the outside, appears to be half way through a wall.

A short distance further along you'll find the Vigne du Clos Montmartre, one of the tiny vineyards that are dotted around the capital. There is a belief that vineyards have existed on Montmartre's hill for over 1000 years. However, the current vineyard dates back to the 1930s, which it was first planted. Every year it produces over 1000 bottles of wine of the highest quality and honors a proud tradition that has been carried on for generations. In addition to its windmill, Montmartre has a number of traditional elements. As another characteristic of Montmartre, its windmill are another part of it's traditional character. It was built in 1717, just before the land was all fields (and vineyards) and now it has been converted into a restaurant. By contrast, the Moulin Blute-Fin in the St. wine region was built in 1622 and is still operational to this day.

The number of these kinds of windmills used to be much higher, but today there are only two remaining. It is true that they decided to name the cafe after them, and in case you were wondering, it is indeed true. Located in the heart of Paris , one of the 12% of public spaces named after a woman in the city, is the beautiful place called Dalida. In the year 1960, Dalida was a singer born of the parents of Italian descent in Egypt. Millions of albums sold over the course of her career, she was one of the most successful recording of all time.

45

13

Notre-Dame

I t is a medieval Gothic cathedral that has been recognized as one of the world's most famous buildings for centuries. Located in the middle of Paris, on an island called La Cite, it is considered to be one of the most picturesque islands in the world. As one of the oldest cathedrals in the world, this cathedral is filled with Gothic elements and architectural details that make it an interesting place to be when visiting. Napoleon saved the cathedral from destruction during the French Revolution and from being destroyed during the Revolutionary War that followed, but the cathedral was mangled during the French Revolution. He was crowned emperor in the cathedral on the day that he became emperor of France.

This cathedral is known throughout the world for its famous story about the Hunchback of Notre Dame. In the 16th and 17th centuries, the nearby Conciergerie was a prison and a medieval royal palace. However, today it is used mainly as a court of law, with a number of other significant functions. It is also worth mentioning that Marie Antoinette was imprisoned in this prison for the last time. It would be easy to imagine how life must have been centuries ago if you were to take a stroll around the historic streets of the island.

14

Catacombs of Paris

E xplore the Catacombs of Paris, a shadowland of underground tunnels and galleries beneath the busy Parisian streets from above, to discover the impressive underground of Paris. Known as the catacomb, this ossuary dates back to the 18th century.

In this era, the remains of over six million people were moved to the tunnel network of former stone mines to reduce the number of cemeteries in Paris. During a visit to this historical underground, you will see the signs of the streets you are under as you walk through the tunnels. In addition, you will see the names of the original cemetery locations from where the remains were originally removed.

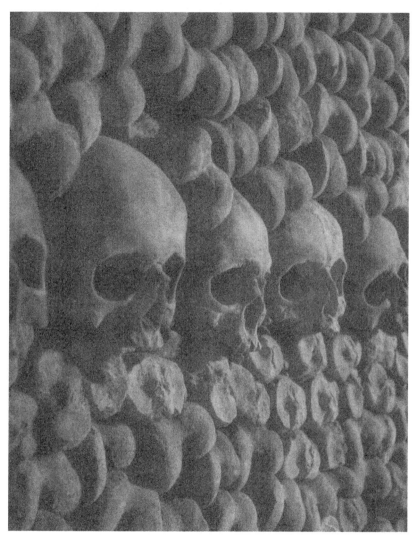

Catacombs of Paris

15

Eiffel Tower

The famous Eiffel Tower is one of the most popular and most recognized world attractions. The Eiffel Tower is the symbol of Paris. As said earlier the Eiffel Tower is about 324 meters high making it the tallest structure in all of Paris.

Construction began in 1889 by the company owned by the engineer Gustave Eiffel as the entrance to the 1889 world's fair and was originally slated for demolition afterward. If you do not like taking the elevator, you can climb the 674 stairs to reach the second floor of the tower. In my experience, many people prefer elevators because they are easier to use and require less effort.

Eiffel Tower

16

Museums

Paris has several hundred museums. There is no doubt that the Louver is Paris' most impressive museum. One of the world's largest art museums, it houses permanent exhibits of works by some of the world's most famous artists, including Leonardo da Vinci's Mona Lisa.

Upon entering the tour, you will be greeted by an impressive glass pyramid. France's military history is represented by many buildings and monuments at Les Invalides, including Napoleon's tomb. Europe's largest museum of modern art is located at the Pompidou Center, designed in the style of high-tech architecture.

Also, don't forget to see the nearby Stravinsky Fountain. A huge collection of impressionist and post-impressionist masterpieces can be found at the Musee d'Orsay, located in a former railway station. You can learn more.

Louvre Museum

What to see in the Louvre Museum -

Mona Lisa - Painted by Leonardo Da Vinci

When you visit the Louvre, you cannot miss Leonardo da Vinci's most famous work of art. However, you should prepare yourself for the crowds that surround it. In addition to being one of the most recognizable paintings in the world, the Mona Lisa is also known as Venus de Milo. She appears elusive and is sought after by many due to her guarded identity and shy smile. Prepare to wait in line to see this famous lady, as many people hope to see her. You don't want to run out of time while waiting for her later in the exhibit, so be sure to make her your first stop at the exhibit.

Winged Victory

Created around 190 BC, this wingless sculpture is another Hellenistic relic. Possibly commissioned by the Rhodesians to commission a naval victory, the wing goddess of victory was a religious offering. As Nike of Samothrace, this sculpture is often depicted on ships' bows completely drenched in seawater. Her crossed legs are blown by the breeze, revealing her nude female form beneath clinging fabrics.

The Great Sphinx

The lion-headed treasure pays homage to the revered relationship between the sun god and the ancient Egyptian king, which was symbolized by the treasure's lion body and human head. Several Pharaohs' names were inscribed on the Sphinx discovered in 1825 in the Temple of Amun ruins. One of the largest Sphinx figures outside of Egypt, it is believed to be the largest outside of Egypt.

Venus de Milo

This famous sculpture, which is made of marble and was carved from a single rock, is actually shrouded in mystery. It is actually a bit of a mystery in itself. According to some researchers, she might have been born as early as 100 BC and was supposed to resemble Aphrodite, a goddess worshipped by the people living on the island of Melos (which is known as Milos today) back then when she was born, and was meant to evoke the image of Aphrodite. A replica of a sculpture from even earlier in time is likely to have served as the inspiration for this statue, according to historians. Although it exhibits many typical aspects of the period in which it was created, it is not a common artifact. Immediately upon noticing her thin veneer of cloth on her draped clothing, they suspected that the woman might be a fake due to her small, exposed breasts on her clothing. My identity is a fictional one. Her missing arms are also a famous fact about her; it has been noted that she has been described as having a lack of arms before. In addition to the possibility that she once held a mirror, a shield, or even an apple, some scholars believe that there are also other theories that have been suggested.

17

Champs-Elysees

One of the world's most recognizable avenues, the Avenue des Champs-Elysees is a 1.2-mile-long street located in the center of Paris. It features numerous luxury shops, theaters, and cafes. Champs-Elysée is the location of the annual Bastille Day military parade and the finish line of the Tour de France cycling race.

Before it became a fashionable avenue in the late 18th century, the location was mostly occupied by fields and gardens. On the west side, the Champs-Elysees ends with the Arc de Triomphe, commissioned by Napoleon.

Champs-Elysees

18

Parks and Gardens

I n Paris, there are a lot of beautiful city parks and gardens. There are many activities you can enjoy here, including walking, jogging, reading, or simply soaking up the atmosphere and experiencing the Parisian culture. The Tuileries Garden, located next to the Louver Museum, is one of the most gorgeous gardens in Paris.

During the 19th and 20th centuries, Parisians used this place to meet. French senators meet at the Luxembourg Palace in the Luxembourg Gardens, which were created in 1612. With lakes, gardens, zoos, botanical gardens, a castle, and other attractions, the Bois de Vincennes is the largest public park in the city. In addition to the parks listed above, Paris offers many more.

Tuileries Garden

19

Pere Lachaise Cemetery

I t is without a doubt that the Pere Lachaise Cemetery is one of the largest cemeteries in Paris and one of the most popular cemeteries in the world. This has been so for generations. It has been around since the early 1800s when it was established. The cemetery is said to contain the graves of Edith Piaf, Jim Morrison, Oscar Wilde, as well as other famous people who have been buried there.

There are a lot of streets in this enormous over 100-acre cemetery, and it's worth your time to explore the many Gothic graves, burial chambers, and ancient mausoleums that are located there. It is worth noting that there are numerous burial plots in the cemetery.

Pere Lachaise Cemetery

20

La Defense Business District

Paris' largest business district is La Defense, home to some of the city's tallest buildings, as well as a large mall with restaurants and cinemas. In La Defense stands the 111-meter-tall Grande Arche, a modern architectural masterpiece mimicking the Arc de Triomphe.

There is a symmetrical alignment between the Arc de Triomphe and the top of the building itself viewed from the observation deck on the top floor of the building. This is over two miles away.

La Defense Business District

21

Versailles

L astly, the Palace of Versailles is an impressive royal residence of the king of France from the late 1600s to the late 1700s until the start of the French Revolution. UNESCO has designated the Château de Versailles as a world heritage site.

It is located about 12 miles (20 km) from Paris. The visit offers an insight into the luxurious lifestyle of French royalty before the French Revolution. You'll discover the Royal Opera House and the expansive Gardens of Versailles as you stroll through the Royal Hall of Mirrors.

Versailles

22

What To Eat in Paris:

I t is well known that when you are visiting the city of Paris, it is not just about the sights, but also about the food you eat. Breakfast can be found in boulangeries, where fresh croissants and baguettes can be purchased for a small price. Lunch and dinner can both be enjoyed in a bistro or a brasserie, both of which are excellent choices.

Coq au vin

There are many classic French dishes that cannot be missed when you eat in Paris, including onion soup, steak fries, and coq au vin. There are many street vendors here that sell crepes, which are a delicious quick snack if you're on the go.

For something sweet, try one of our delicious macarons, a delicious piece of rich chocolate, or an old-fashioned French creme brulee if you are craving something sweet. There are a number of restaurants in the city that provide top-quality food in a variety of settings, so you can choose whether you want something formal or casual.

There are many Michelin-starred restaurants in Paris to choose from if you're in the mood for a special dining experience, so be sure to check out one. You can find some of the finest restaurants in Paris, such as Guy Savoy, L Atelier de Joel Robuchon, and Le Bernardin, among many others.

23

Best Restaurants to Visit in Paris

There is no doubt that Paris is home to some of the world's most delicious cuisines. Pink Mamma is one of those excellent restaurants I recommend you visit. In my opinion, this restaurant definitely exceeded my expectations. At first, I thought the food couldn't be that wonderful because it's hyped up and maybe people are more attracted to the decor than the food. Obviously, I was wrong in a very large way. It is a fact that the truffle pasta they served was simply one of the most delicious pastas I have ever eaten in my whole life! My experience with it was very pleasant, and I was very happy with it. You should make sure that you get a seat at the top of the restaurant, if even by chance you happen to go to this restaurant. And make sure that you make reservations well in advance.

If you're wondering which restaurant is the most recommended in Paris, then Giorgio would be the answer. A retro pink disco theme is incorporated into the design of this specific restaurant. There is no doubt that you will be amazed by the interior. Throughout the room there are tons of mirrors everywhere, a lot of blue lighting, and there are also a lot of amazing strip designs as well. These designs give an amazing touch. The pizza that they serve there is one of the most delicious that you can find in any restaurant in Paris. Despite the fact that it was fluffy and crisp at the same time, it had a delightful texture. They also offer the most delicious tiramisu soup.

In terms of restaurants, you definitely need to visit Brasserie Dubillot. It's a traditional French restaurant where you'll find delicious dishes like delicious steaks. This is an amazing place where you can chill and relax with your partner or friends, hang out and catch up. Typically, people arrive around 5pm or 6pm for happy hour, then chill till dinner time.

There are other small restaurants you can stop by to get a quick meal such as Yellow Tucan for coffee, Perrier Herme for macarons, Baked Bastards for Boulangerie, Café de Flore for French Café, Shangri La Paris for drinks, Aki Café for Japanese curry, and Surpriz- Berliner Kebab for the most delicious takeout. Kaf Kaf is one of the city's top brunch restaurants. This is a great brunch spot. Inside they serve California-inspired cuisine. The décor is minimal however. They also serve the charcoal egg avocado burger which was my favorite.

24

If You Happen Travel Outside the City of Paris and Explore the Rest of France

A s a result of its excellent tourist attractions, France ranks as one of the top tourist destinations in the world, not only in Europe, but also worldwide. There are millions of tourists who visit France every year, particularly Paris, due to its rich cultural heritage.

There are a lot of attractions in the city, including stunning architecture, breathtaking scenery, sophisticated culture, fine wines, and delicious cuisine, so there is surely something for everyone.

The city of Paris is one of the most popular cities in France, but there are many other places that you can visit besides Paris. In order to help you make the most of your time in the countryside, we have put together a list of the top places you can check out.

France Countryside

25

Lyon, France

Lyon, France

Among Lyon's World Heritage Sites are a historic Renaissance old town, Roman ruins, historic industrial districts, fine dining restaurants, a museum commemorating the pioneering Lumiere brothers, and ancient Roman theaters. Several Roman sites have been discovered at Lyon's pilgrimage site, Fourviere Basilica.

Lyon's north tower boasts some of the most picturesque views in the city, and inside are lavish interiors and sacred art museums. In addition to providing ingredients for professional chefs, Lyon also has several markets where consumers can purchase their food.

Food markets such as Saint-Antoine, La Croix-Rousse, or Les Halles de Lyon are among the places you can nibble your way through. Throughout the summer, Lyon's two Roman theaters host a music and arts festival, which are examples of stone-tiered outdoor theaters of the Roman Empire.

26

Nice, France

Nice, France

This new Unesco is known for its sunny climes, gorgeous beaches, and colorful architecture. In addition to its art and culture, the city offers many world-class attractions and activities.

Take a stroll along the Promenade des Anglais in Nice when you're there. It's more than just a grand walkway. Embraced by regal 19th-century palaces on its eastern side, the promenade bends for 7 km.

Aside from the ancient alleyways and colorful facades of Nice's old town, you should also visit the city's typical Mediterranean shutters and shady alleyways. When you visit the old town of Nice, I also recommend you see Rossetti Square. Here the magnificent Saint Reparata Cathedral is located in Saint Francis Square and its small market.

27

Cannes, France

Cannes, France

C annes is a must-see when visiting the French Riviera. There is more to Cannes than just the Cannes Film Festival and

A-list actors. Visiting this beautiful city means that you can leave Cannes every morning and travel through Provence without ever leaving. This covered market offers seasonal produce from all over the south of France, as well as regional flavors. Observing the city's daily life can be rare in this city, which makes it a favorite among locals.

Fruit, flowers, and aromatic herbs can be found on the menu, as well as exquisite confectionery, truffles, and gourmet olive oils. A popular avenue on the French Riviera is the Boulevard de la Croisette. It is here that Cannes' tourist activity centers around palm-lined boulevards. There are luxurious Belle Epoque villas, upscale boutiques, and the legendary Carlton Cannes along the Boulevard de la Croisette.

Designed by Charles Dalmas, this is a masterpiece of Art Nouveau architecture. The vast majority of Cannes is sleek and modern, but Le Suquet is quite the opposite. It is one of the most picturesque neighborhoods in Cannes and one of the oldest neighborhoods in the city.

With pastel-colored buildings that have stood since the 18th and 19th centuries, you can stroll through the streets of the city while admiring the panoramic views above you. It was once a Roman settlement. Today, the Suquet consists of narrow ascending streets, underground bars, and family restaurants. This neighborhood is worth exploring if you have a little time to spare.

28

Mont Saint Michel

Mont Saint Michel

L ike a beacon rising from the sea, Mont Saint-Michel is a sight to behold. In Normandy, Mont Saint-Michel is a top tourist attraction and a UNESCO World Heritage Site. In the center of the island is the Grande Rue, which is its main street.

Upon entering the island's main gate, it begins immediately, so you won't miss it. Several restaurants and souvenir shops are located here, so the street is often crowded. You'll feel like you're walking back in time as you stroll down this cobblestone street. I highly recommend visiting the island's abbey, as it is by far one of the most enjoyable things to do.

Despite centuries of being a place of worship, prayer, and pilgrimage, today the abbey receives a growing number of tourists. You won't be able to experience Mount Saint Michel if you don't visit the abbey. Upon entering the halls, corridors, and courtyards, you will be awed by the magnificent architecture.

For more information, you can use Yelp and TripAdvisor. This is where you can find some of the cheapest deals on hotel accommodations, flights, and the most affordable car rentals in France.

29

Toulouse, France

Toulouse, France

I ts pleasant atmosphere, despite being a major industrial city, makes Toulouse a comfortable city with a laid-back vibe. Among its nicknames is "the pink city", which refers to the city of Toulouse. There are so many magnificent buildings in the city that are built of pinkish brick. This gives the cityscape an unparalleled look, as most buildings in the city are made from this kind of brick.

The history of Toulouse can be traced back to this beautiful, well-preserved square that is at the heart of the city. You can view the iconic pink stone former Grande Palace from many of the cafes lining the street. The latter is one of the most spectacular structures I have ever seen.

It is renowned for its magnificent setting for many of the world's most famous operas. Once again, it plays host to the city's theater, which is also a fittingly grand location for the city's prestigious operas.

On the medieval pilgrimage route from Santiago de Compostela to the Holy Land in Spain, one of the most notable and magnificent churches is the Basilica of Saint-Sernin. The Basilica of Saint Andrew is regarded as Europe's largest church, which was built in the 11th to 13th centuries. At its current size, it costs around $17 million to maintain.

30

Strasbourg, France

Strasbourg, France

The Alsace region is stunning, and Strasburg is no exception. France and Germany have been in a centuries-long tug-of-war over it, and the sandstone there makes it even more captivating and captivating. The Strasbourg Cathedral remains the tallest surviving medieval structure in the world.

It was the tallest building in the world during the medieval era. There are several Romanesque and Neo-Gothic Gothic churches in addition to the stunning cathedral. The downtown area is home to a variety of architectural styles, including Baroque, Wilhelmina, and contemporary. Strasbourg's Rohan Place is one of the city's most iconic buildings.

The building dates from the early part of the 18th century and represents a wonderful example of French architecture in the 18th century. This palace houses a number of museums that are dedicated to archaeology and the fine arts.

31

Resources

GetYourGuide. (n.d.). *The BEST Paris Tours and Things to Do in 2022 - FREE Cancellation.* Retrieved October 29, 2022, from https://www.getyourguide.com/-116/?cmp=ga

The Blonde Abroad. (2022, August 11). *The Ultimate Paris Travel Guide* •. https://www.theblondeabroad.com/ultimate-paris-travel-guide/

Picard, S. (2022, September 6). *Famous Food in Paris: The 7 Local Bites You Have to Try - Devour Paris.* Devour Tours. https://devourtours.com/blog/famous-food-in-paris/?cnt=US

GetYourGuide. (n.d.-a). *The BEST Lyon Tours and Things to Do in 2022 - FREE Cancellation.* Retrieved October 29, 2022, from https://www.getyourguide.com/-1295/?cmp=ga

The Editors of Encyclopedia Britannica. (2022, September 7). *Nice | History, Geography, & Points of Interest.* Encyclopedia Britannica. https://www.britannica.com/place/Nice

Ledsom, A. (2018, May 18). *The Top Unmissable Things to Do in Cannes, France*. Culture Trip. https://theculturetrip.com/europe/france/articl es/20-unmissable-attractions-in-cannes/

Visit the Mont-Saint-Michel and its Bay in Normandy. (2021, December 1). Normandy Tourism, France. https://en.normandie-tourisme.fr/ unmissable-sites/the-mont-saint-michel/

Toulouse - a capital city in southwest France. (n.d.). Retrieved October 29, 2022, from https://about-france.com/cities/toulouse.htm

Levine, I. S. (2018, September 25). *6 Reasons To Visit Strasbourg, France: Cradle Of Alsatian Culture*. Forbes. https://www.forbes.com/sites/iren elevine/2018/09/25/6-reasons-to-visit-strasbourg-france-cradle-of-a lsatian-culture/?sh=49e5d88f5539

Saward, B. (2022, June 5). *Top 10 Places in the French Countryside*. World of Wanderlust. https://worldofwanderlust.com/top-10-places-in-the-french-countryside/

Made in United States
Orlando, FL
06 December 2022

25609919R00059